World Book, Inc.
233 N. Michigan Avenue
Chicago, IL 60601
U.S.A.

For information about other World Book publications,
visit our website at www.worldbook.com
or call 1-800-WORLDBK (967-5325).
For information about sales to schools and libraries,
call 1-800-975-3250 (United States),
or 1-800-837-5365 (Canada).

Library of Congress Cataloging-in-Publication Data

Addition.

   pages cm. -- (Building blocks of mathematics)
   Summary: "A graphic nonfiction volume that
introduces critical basic addition concepts"--
Provided by publisher.
   Includes index.
   ISBN 978-0-7166-1432-6 -- ISBN 978-0-7166-1473-9
(pbk.)
   1. Addition--Comic books, strips, etc.--Juvenile
literature. 2. Graphic novels. I. World Book, Inc.
QA115.A336 2013
513.2'11--dc23
                         2012031035

Building Blocks of Mathematics
ISBN: 978-0-7166-1431-9 (set, hc.)

Printed in China by Shenzhen Donnelley
Printing Co., Ltd., Guangdong Province
2nd printing October 2013

Acknowledgments:
Created by Samuel Hiti and Joseph Midthun
Art by Samuel Hiti
Written by Joseph Midthun
Special thanks to Anita Wager, Hala
Ghousseini, and Syril McNally.

STAFF
Executive Committee
President: Donald D. Keller
Vice President and Editor in Chief:
   Paul A. Kobasa
Vice President, Sales & Marketing:
   Sean Lockwood
Vice President, International: Richard Flower
Director, Human Resources: Bev Ecker

Editorial
Manager, Series and Trade: Cassie Mayer
Writer and Letterer: Joseph Midthun
Manager, Contracts & Compliance
   (Rights & Permissions): Loranne K. Shields

Manufacturing/Pre-Press
Director: Carma Fazio
Manufacturing Manager: Steven Hueppchen
Production/Technology Manager:
   Anne Fritzinger
Proofreader: Emilie Schrage

Graphics and Design
Senior Manager, Graphics and Design: Tom Evans
Coordinator, Design Development and
   Production: Brenda B. Tropinski
Book Design: Samuel Hiti

TABLE OF CONTENTS

What Is Addition?........................4

Counting On...........................6

Find the Tens 8

Doubles 12

Making Friendly Numbers 16

More Friendly Numbers 18

Mealtime Addition.....................20

Matching and Counting Up............24

Addition All Around 28

Addition Facts 30

Find Out More..........................31

Note to Educators 32

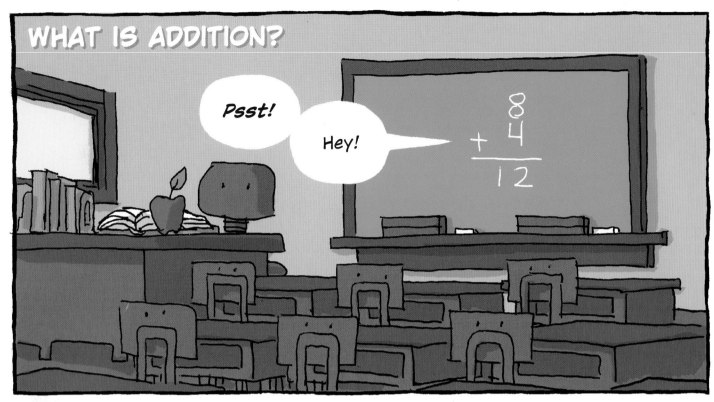

You probably recognize me from around here.

I'm Addition.

I join numbers together!

plop

You can use *me* to describe the world around *you.*

TUMP

You have probably seen me like this:

1 + 2 = 3

Here are 4 red balloons...

...and here are 8 blue balloons.

How many balloons are there all together?

How would you add these numbers?

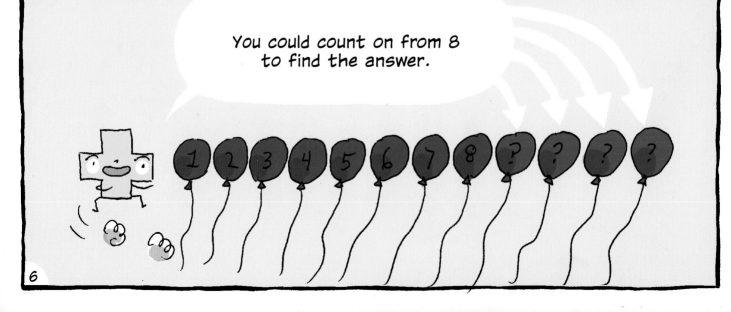

You could count on from 8 to find the answer.

Or you could add 8 + 2 to make a group of 10.

Then add the remaining ones to find the answer.

ZIP

ZOOP

We have 1 ten and 2 ones. How much does that equal?

10 + 2 = 12!

Let's find some more things to add!

ZOOM

TUMP

Ants and aphids!

I love insects!

Let's count the ants first.

How many are there?

12!

Now let's count the aphids!

15!

How many insects are there all together?

Um.   Ah?

Let's see if we can add the same numbers a different way.

First, let's add the ones.

How much is that?

Two more than 5 equals...

SEVEN!

DOUBLES

Knowing doubles can help you add fast!

Have you ever heard of doubles?

Double 1 is the same as 2.

Double 2 is the same as 4.

Double 3 is the same as 6.

Double 4 is the same as 8.

Eek!

Double 5 is the same as 10.

Double 6 is the same as 12.

Double 7 is the same as 14.

Double 8 is the same as 16.

Double 9 is the same as 18.

Double 10 is the same as 20!

Let's use doubles to figure out what 5 + 6 equals...

TUMP   TUMP

It's *double 5* plus 1 more.

Snap

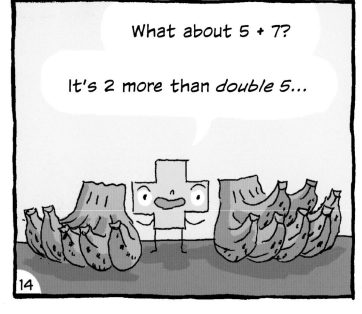

What about 5 + 7?

It's 2 more than *double 5*...

...or the same as *double 6!*

Snap   Snap

They're tough to add up in your head!

Sometimes numbers can seem unfriendly.

But we can regroup numbers to make them friendlier.

How about you give us an example, wise guy?

Okay.

Say we want to add a row of 11 seeds to this other row of 9 seeds.

Let's find out how many seeds we'll have in all.

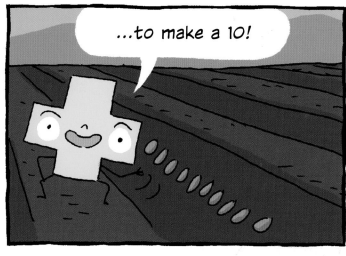

MORE FRIENDLY NUMBERS

Look at these two numbers!

Can you add them in your head?

18 is close to 20, so why don't we move 2 ones from 23 over here to 18?

What if you think of the numbers as something else?

Like 23 footballs and 18 tennis balls?

Let's regroup!

23

18

18 and 2 is the same as 20.

After regrouping, you have 20 and 20...

...and 1!

20 and 20 equals 40!

Now, all you have to do is solve 40+1!

You can do that in your head!

We didn't change the amount we were adding. We just regrouped the numbers!

Fun, huh?!

19

Every day, you need to eat 21 fish in order to survive.

Yum!

Uh oh.

Yeesh!

CHOMP CHOMP CHOMP CHOMP CHOMP CHOMP

Today, you've already eaten 10 fish.

How many more fish do you need to eat today?

Let's take a closer look and figure it out...

Hmm.

You know you need to eat 21 fish.

And you know you've already eaten 10.

What if you make a jump of 10?

That's right, *double 10!*

Let's try! It's okay if we make a mistake...

Double 10 equals 20.

10 + 10 = 20!

Close, but not perfect...

We're still 1 away from 21.

Hmm.

So, I need to eat 10 fish + 1 fish?

Now, you're getting there!

There are 15 pelicans in this flock...

...and there are 23 gulls in this flock.

How many more birds are there in the flock of gulls?

Let's compare by matching up the equal amounts.

Math doesn't make the world go 'round, but it does help you describe it.

And, if you can describe the world around you...

...let's just say, the possibilities are **ENDLESS!**

If you ever come across a problem you can't solve, don't hold it in...

LET IT OUT!

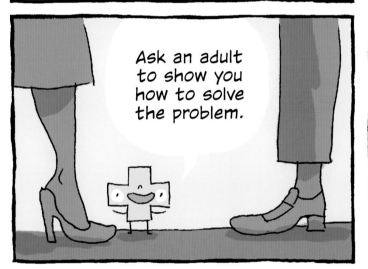

Ask an adult to show you how to solve the problem.

If you keep at it, maybe some day you can show someone else how to solve it!

STAY POSITIVE!

I'm Addition!

ADDITION FACTS

This table can help you add as easy as 1, 2, 3!
It can also help you learn your addition facts.

HERE'S HOW IT WORKS:

1. Choose a number from the column on the left.
2. Then choose a number from the top row of the table.
3. Find the point where the two numbers meet.

YOU'VE FOUND THE TOTAL OF THE TWO NUMBERS!

+	0	1	2	3	4	5	6	7	8	9	10
0	0	1	2	3	4	5	6	7	8	9	10
1	1	2	3	4	5	6	7	8	9	10	11
2	2	3	4	5	6	7	8	9	10	11	12
3	3	4	5	6	7	8	9	10	11	12	13
4	4	5	6	7	8	9	10	11	12	13	14
5	5	6	7	8	9	10	11	12	13	14	15
6	6	7	8	9	10	11	12	13	14	15	16
7	7	8	9	10	11	12	13	14	15	16	17
8	8	9	10	11	12	13	14	15	16	17	18
9	9	10	11	12	13	14	15	16	17	18	19
10	10	11	12	13	14	15	16	17	18	19	20

FOR EXAMPLE:

1 + 0 = 1; 1 + 2 = 3; 1 + 3 = 4; and so on!